ISBN-13: 978-1-4234-1030-0
ISBN-10: 1-4234-1030-0

HAL•LEONARD®
CORPORATION
7777 W. BLUEMOUND RD. P.O. BOX 13819 MILWAUKEE, WI 53213

Visit Hal Leonard Online at
www.halleonard.com

BOCK, Jerry (Jerrold Lewis), composer; born New Haven, November 23, 1928; s. George Joseph and Rebecca (Alpert) B.; m. Patricia Faggen, May 28, 1950; children: George Albert, Portia Fane. Student, University of Wisconsin (1945–1949), L.H.D. (hon.), 1985. Writer: score for high school musical, *My Dream*, 1943; score for college musical, *Big as Life*, 1948; songs for TV show "Admiral Broadway Revue," also "Show of Shows," 1949–1951; composer songs, "Camp Tamiment," summers 1950, 1951, 1953 writer: continuity sketches "Mel Torme" show, CBS, 1951, 1952; writing staff: "Kate Smith Hour," 1953–1954; writer: original songs for night club performer, including night club revue *Confetti*; wrote: songs for *Wonders of Manhattan* (honorable mention Cannes Film Festival 1956); composer: music for Broadway show, *Catch a Star*, 1955; *Mr. Wonderful*, 1956; (collaborated with Sheldon Harnick on) *The Body Beautiful*, 1958; *Fiorello!*, 1959 (Pulitzer prize, Drama Critics award, Antoinette Perry award); *Tenderloin*, 1960; *She Loves Me*, (1963); *Fiddler on the Roof*, 1964; *The Apple Tree*, 1966; *The Rothschilds*, 1972; London production of *She Loves Me*, 1964, off-Broadway 1982; *Fiddler on the Roof*, 1964 (nine Tonys and best musical of the year); London production of *Fiddler on the Roof*, 1964 (Tony Award®); Warsaw production, 1985, *Fiorello!*; *Goodspeed Opera House*, summer 1985; wrote series of children's songs now published under the title *Sing Something Special*; also recorded album, N.Y. Board of Education, radio broadcasts, 1961. Recipient Johnny Mercer award from Songwriters Hall of Fame, 1990; named to Theatre Hall of Fame, 1990. Member Broadcast Music Inc. 1989–1990—Silver Anniversary production of *Fiddler on the Roof* National Tour, ending in New York Revival; 1989— Jerome Robbins' *Broadway*; 1990—*The Rothschilds* revival. Member of an endowment group at the National Foundation for Advancement in the Arts. Member of the advisory panel for the BMI Foundation. Composed the score for the film, *A Stranger Among Us*; wrote words and music for *The Magic Journey*, *Danny and the Dragon*, *Brandon Finds His Star*, *Pinocchio*, and *Land of Broken Toys* for the Children's Theatre Festival, University of Houston, 2000–2005.

SHELDON HARNICK, born and educated in Chicago, moved to New York City in the early 1950s to pursue a career as a composer-lyricist for the American musical theater. He contributed numbers to several revues of the era including *New Faces of 1952* (the hilarious "Boston Beguine") and John Murray Anderson's *Almanac* (the sardonic "Merry Minuet"). In 1958, he began a collaboration with composer Jerry Bock to write the Broadway musical *The Body Beautiful*. The team of Bock and Harnick went on to write *Fiorello!*, *Tenderloin*, *She Loves Me*, *Fiddler on the Roof*, *The Apple Tree*, and *The Rothschilds*. Other collaborations include *Rex* (Richard Rodgers), *A Christmas Carol* (Michel Legrand), *A Wonderful Life* (Joe Raposo), and *The Phantom Tollbooth* (Arnold Black and co-librettist Norton Juster). For *Dragons*, Mr. Harnick provided music and book as well as lyrics. With Cy Coleman, he contributed songs to the films *The Heartbreak Kid* and *Blame It on Rio*, and with Michel Legrand he wrote the score for the animated film *Aaron's Magic Village*.

Mr. Harnick, at one time a professional violinist, is no stranger to the realm of opera and operetta. Among his many translations, the most frequently performed are Bizet's *Carmen*, Stravinsky's *L'Histoire du Soldat*, Mozart's *The Goose from Cairo*, and Lehar's *The Merry Widow*. He has provided librettos for *Coyote Tales* with composer Henry Mollicone; *The Audition* with Marvin Hamlisch; three operas with Jack Beeson: *Captain Jinks of the Horse Marines*, *Dr. Heidegger's Fountain of Youth*, and *Cyrano*; and *Love in Two Countries* with composer Thomas Z. Shepard.

Mr. Harnick has won two Tony Awards®, two GRAMMY Awards®, two New York Drama Critics' Circle Awards, three gold records, and a platinum record. In 2005, he and his wife Margery celebrated their fortieth anniversary with their children Beth and Matthew. Mr. Harnick is a long-time member of both the Dramatists Guild and the Songwriters Guild of America.

SHE LOVES ME

CONTENTS

DAYS GONE BY

Words by SHELDON HARNICK
Music by JERRY BOCK

Moderato (Nostalgic)

Young, strong, Oh, I was some-thing in

DAYS GONE BY. With

some girl who just hap-pened to catch

TONIGHT AT EIGHT

Words by SHELDON HARNICK
Music by JERRY BOCK

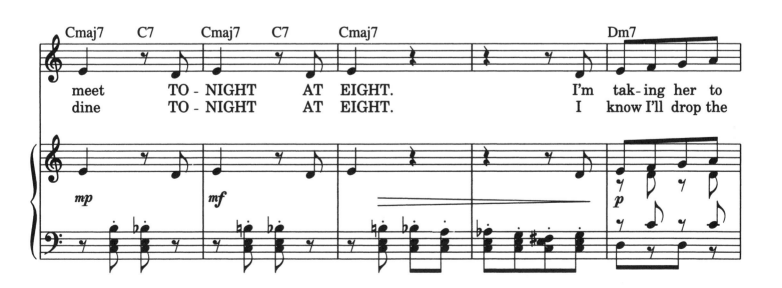

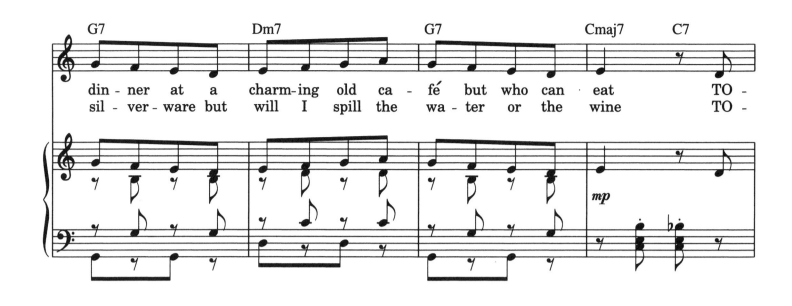

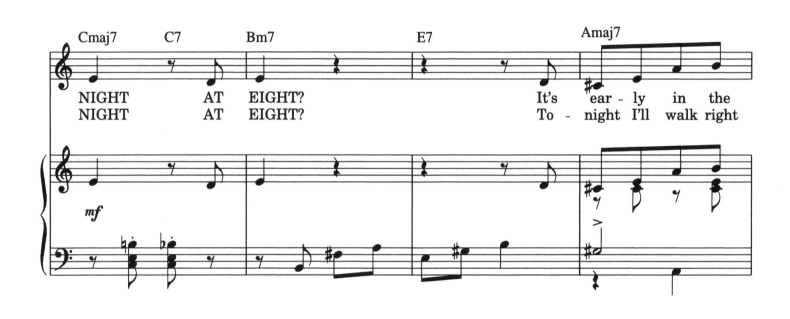

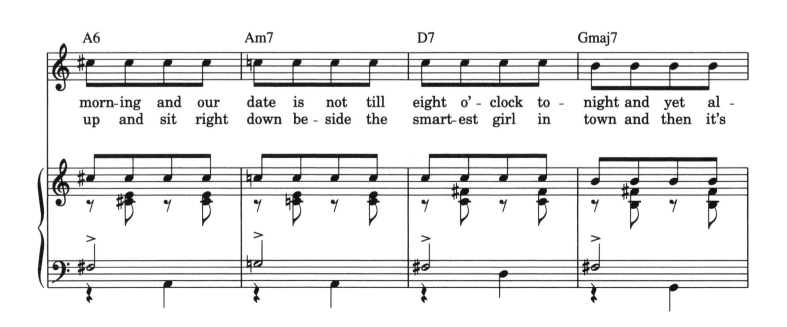

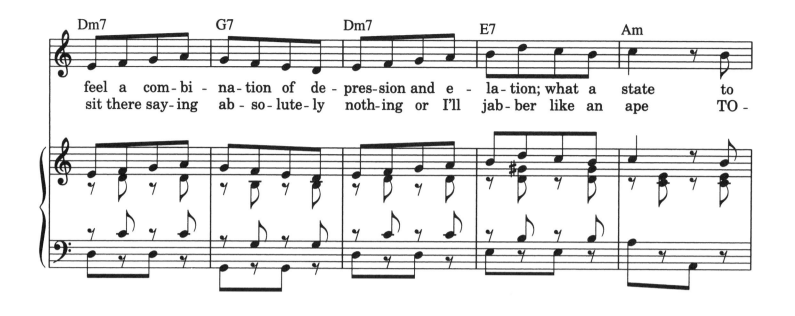

feel a com-bi - na-tion of de-pres-sion and e - la - tion; what a state to
sit there say-ing ab - so-lute-ly noth-ing or I'll jab-ber like an ape TO -

wait 'til eight._____ Three more min - utes,
NIGHT AT EIGHT._____ Two more min - utes,

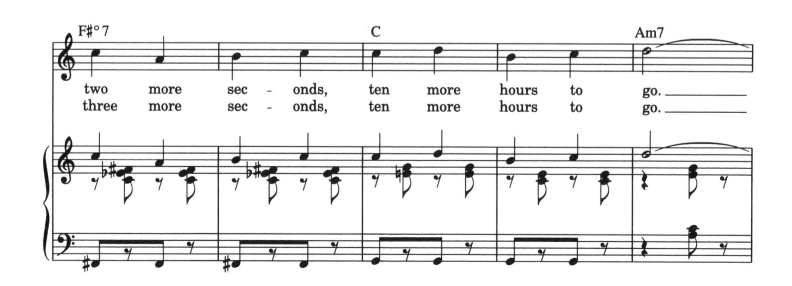

two more sec - onds, ten more hours to go._____
three more sec - onds, ten more hours to go._____

In spite of all I've writ-ten, she may not be ver-y
I'll know when this is done if some-thing's end-ed or be -

smit-ten and my hopes, per-haps, may all col -
gun and if it goes all right, Who knows, I

lapse, *ka - put,* TO - NIGHT AT EIGHT! EIGHT!
might pro - pose TO - NIGHT AT

WILL HE LIKE ME?

Words by SHELDON HARNICK
Music by JERRY BOCK

sees?_____ If he does-n't, will he know e-nough to know_____ that there's

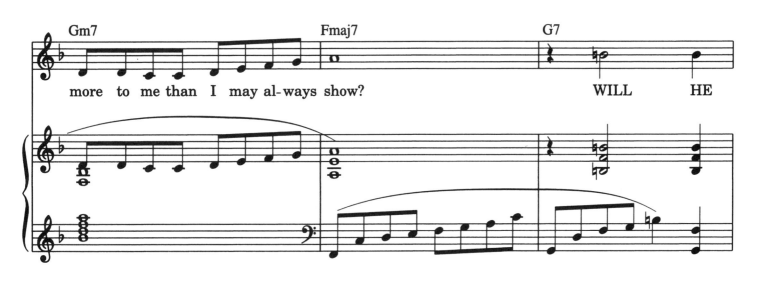

more to me than I may al-ways show? WILL HE

LIKE ME? Will he know that there's a world of

love   wait - ing to warm him?   How I'm hop-ing that his

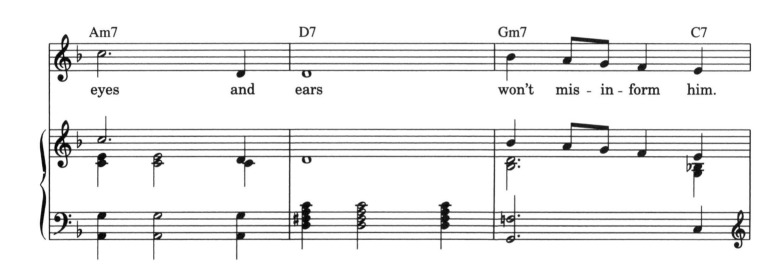

eyes   and   ears   won't mis - in - form him.

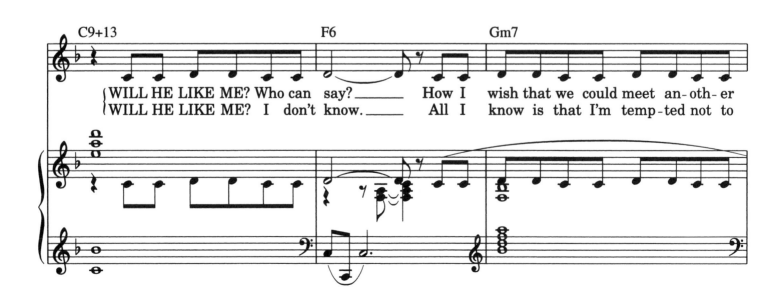

WILL HE LIKE ME? Who can say?_____ How I wish that we could meet an-oth-er
WILL HE LIKE ME? I don't know._____ All I know is that I'm temp-ted not to

day. _____ It's ab - surd for me to car-ry on this way. }
go. _____ It's in - san-i - ty for me to wor-ry so. }

I'll try not to. WILL HE LIKE ME?

To Coda ⊕

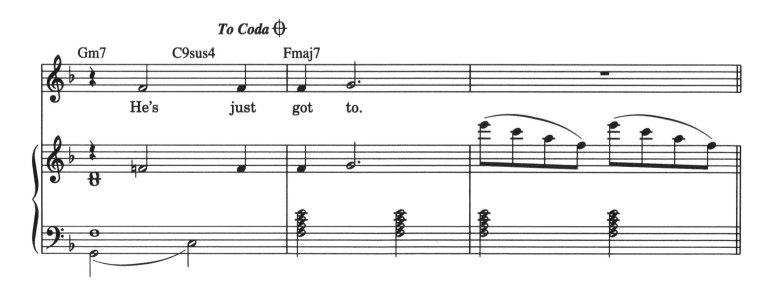

He's just got to.

Interlude

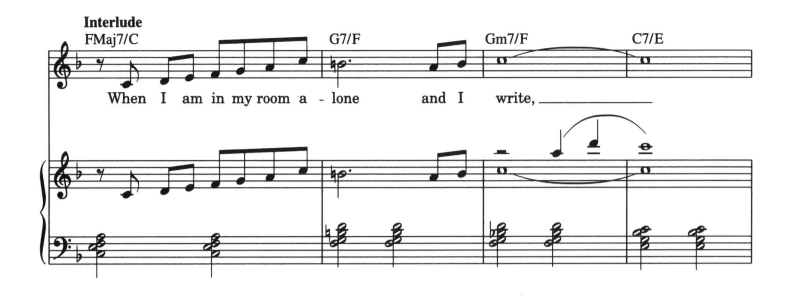

When I am in my room a - lone and I write, _____

Thoughts came eas - i - ly, words come flu - ent - ly then. _____

— That's how it is when I'm a - lone But to -

ILONA

Words by SHELDON HARNICK
Music by JERRY BOCK

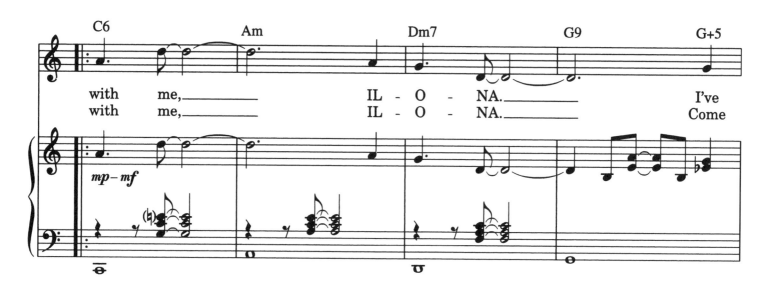

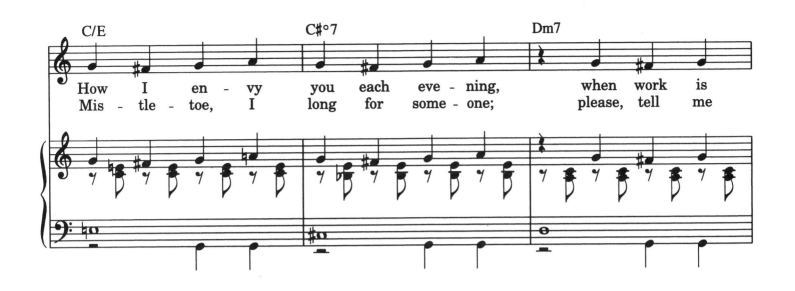

How I en - vy you each eve - ning, when work is
Mis - tle - toe, I long for some - one; please, tell me

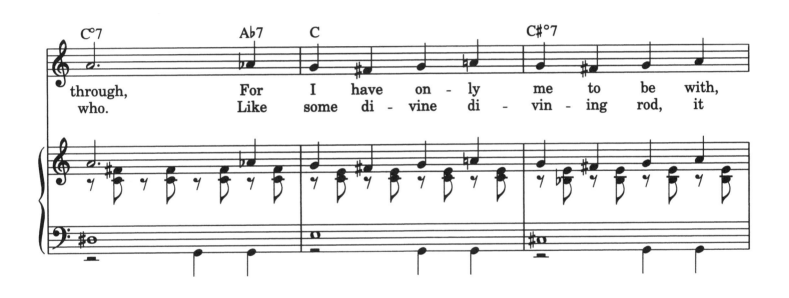

through, For I have on - ly me to be with,
who. Like some di - vine di - vin - ing rod, it

while you have you. With - out you,___
points straight to you. Re - mem - ber,___

(rubato)

a tempo

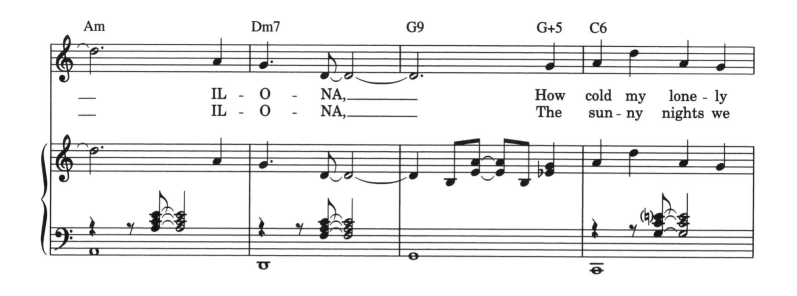

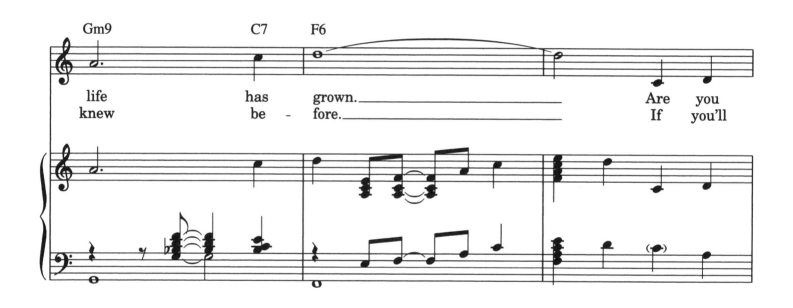

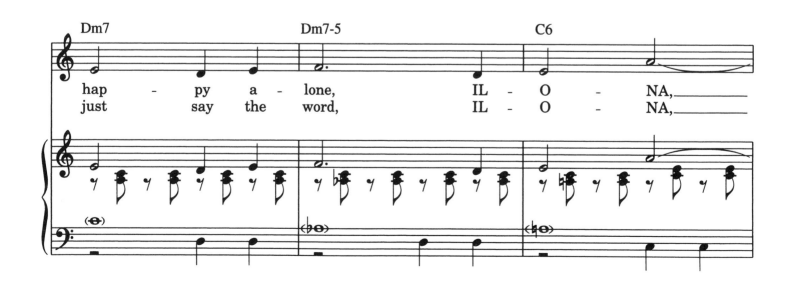

DEAR FRIEND

Words by SHELDON HARNICK
Music by JERRY BOCK

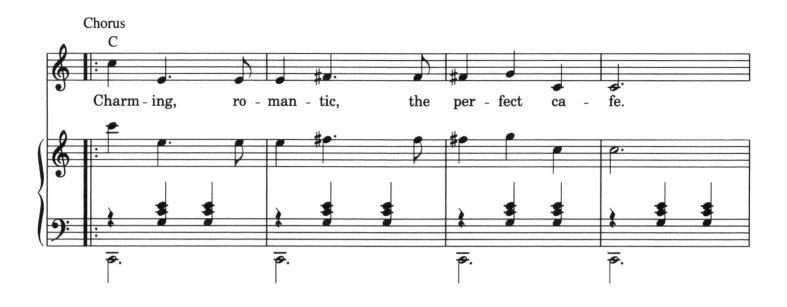

Charm - ing, ro - man - tic, the per - fect ca - fe.

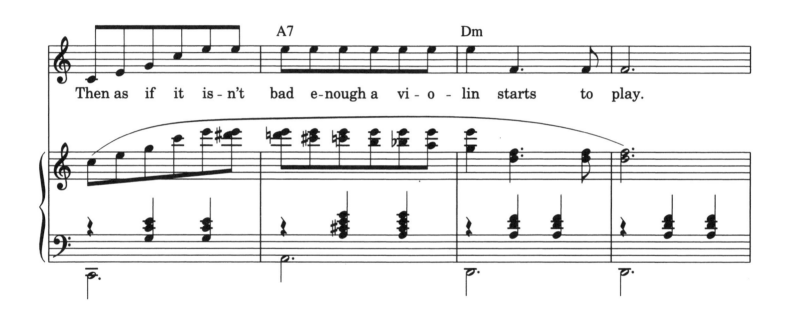

Then as if it is - n't bad e-nough a vi - o - lin starts to play.

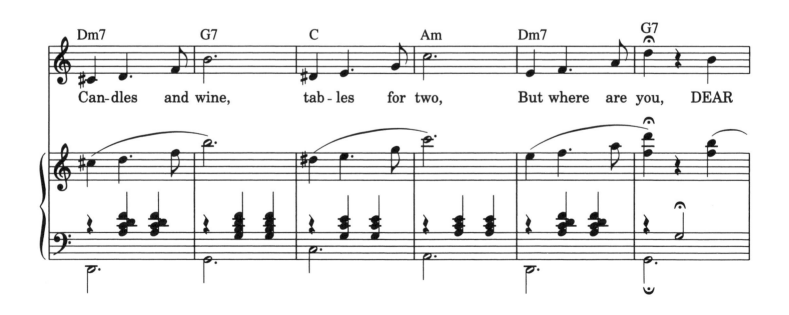

Can - dles and wine, tab - les for two, But where are you, DEAR

FRIEND?   Cou-ples   go past me. (She:) I   see how they look:
(He:) In   worlds of their own,

So dis-creet-ly sym-pa - thet - ic when they see the rose and   the book.
They see noth-ing so un - u - su - al in some-one din - ing   a - lone.

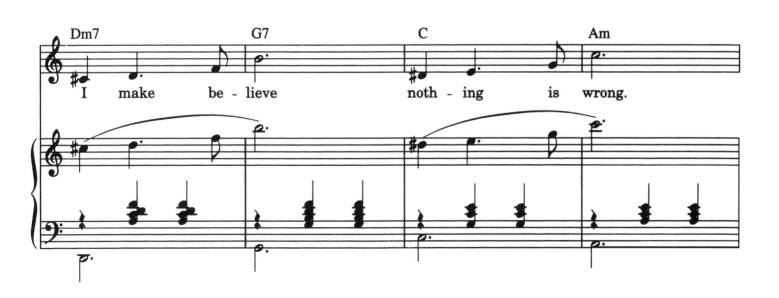

I   make be - lieve   noth - ing   is   wrong.

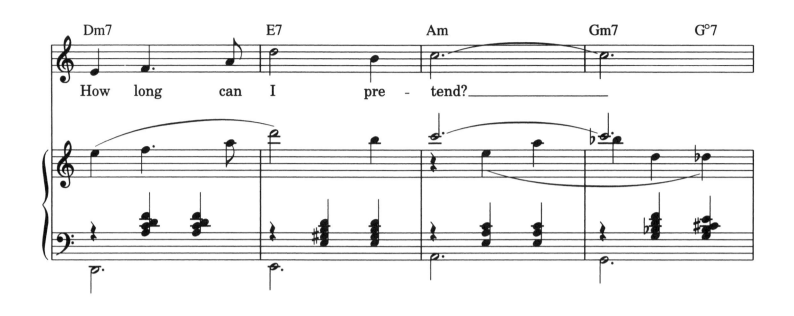

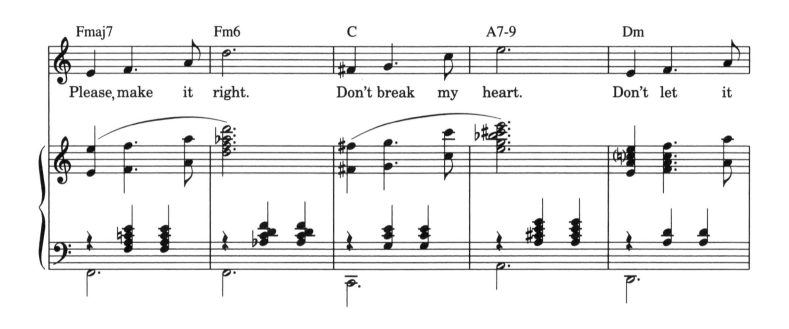

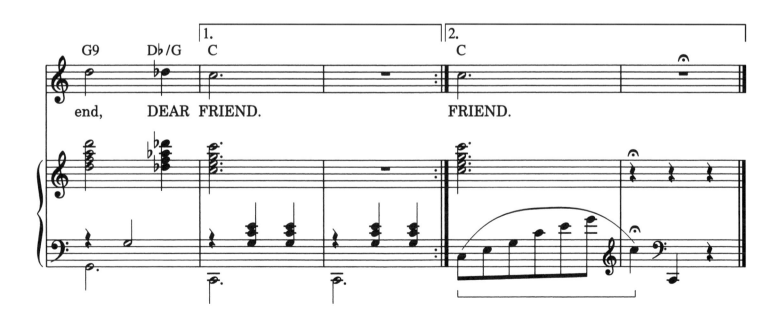

VANILLA ICE CREAM

Words by SHELDON HARNICK
Music by JERRY BOCK

SHE LOVES ME

Words by SHELDON HARNICK
Music by JERRY BOCK

A TRIP TO THE LIBRARY

Words by SHELDON HARNICK
Music by JERRY BOCK

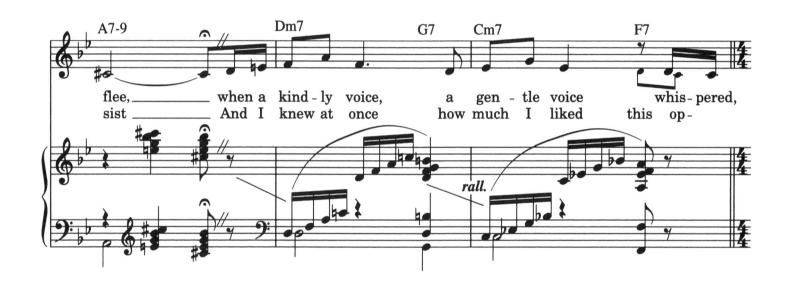

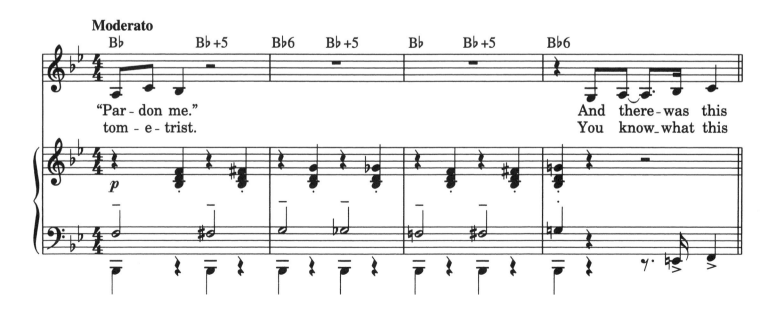

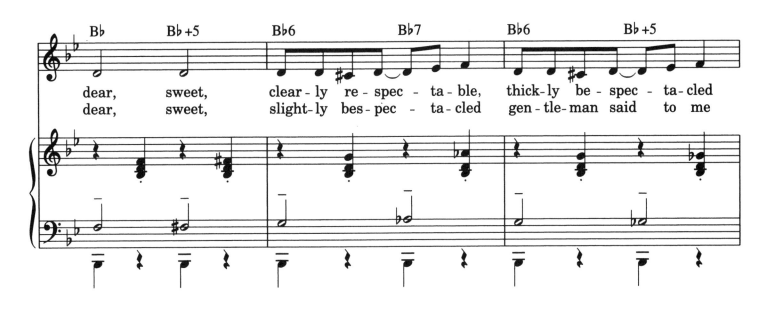

dear, sweet, clear-ly re - spec - ta - ble, thick-ly be - spec - ta - cled
dear, sweet, slight-ly bes - pec - ta - cled gen - tle-man said to me

man Who stood_ by my side and qui - et - ly said _ to me,
next? He said_ he could solve this prob-lem of mine._ I said,

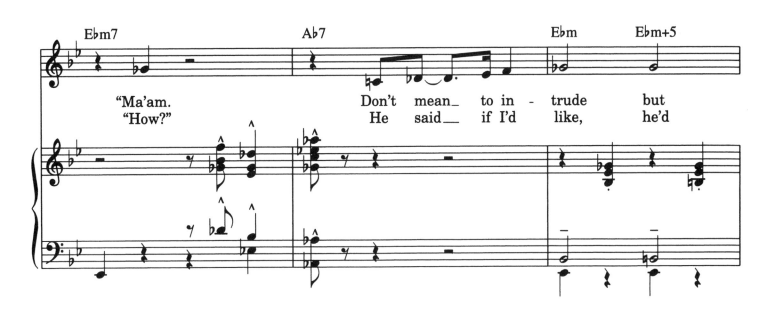

"Ma'am. Don't mean_ to in - trude but
"How?" He said_ if I'd like, he'd

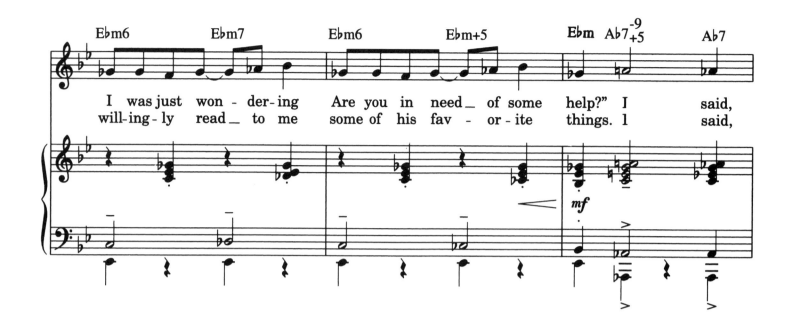

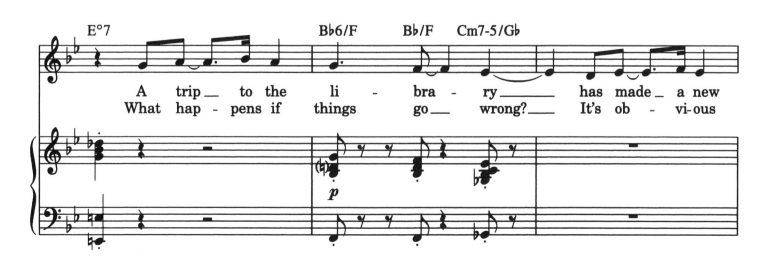

GRAND KNOWING YOU

Words by SHELDON HARNICK
Music by JERRY BOCK

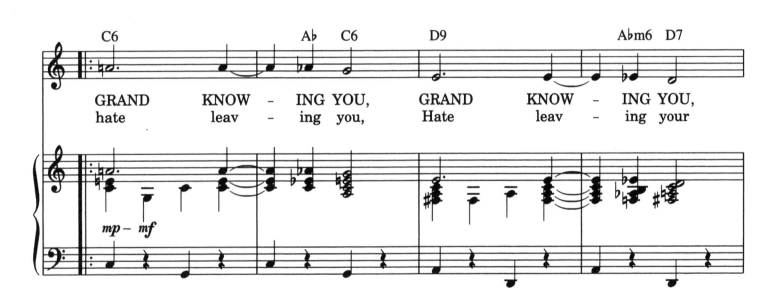

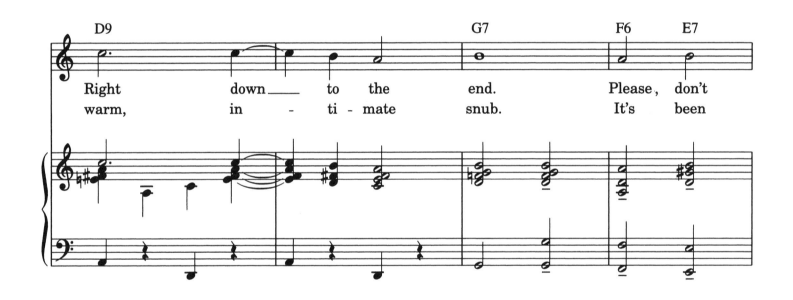

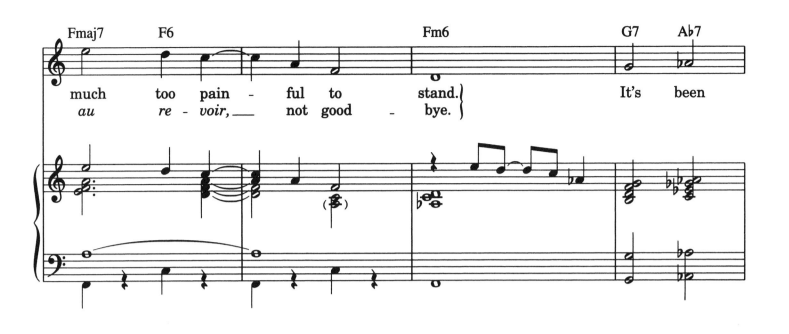